Cutie Pops

Text and Photography by
ELISABETH ANTOINE AND ELIZABETH CUNNINGHAM HERRING

To Paco, Nane, Yves, Mony, and Anne-Marie
for their unwavering love and support.
—Elisabeth Antoine

To Dick, Budgy, Caroline, and Richard
for their love and encouragement.
—Elizabeth Cunningham Herring

Acknowledgments

We would like to thank our families and friends for their support and for tasting and helping us refine our recipes. We are particularly grateful to Caroline Cunningham for her patient and gracious advice.

We would also like to thank the crew at Sellers Publishing, especially Robin Haywood, Jeff Hall, and Charlotte Cromwell.

Published by Sellers Publishing, Inc.
Text and photography copyright © 2013 Elisabeth Antoine & Elizabeth Cunningham Herring
All rights reserved.

Sellers Publishing, Inc.
161 John Roberts Road, South Portland, Maine 04106
Visit our Web site: www.sellerspublishing.com
E-mail: rsp@rsvp.com

ISBN 13: 978-1-4162-0885-3
e-ISBN: 978-1-4162-0905-8
Library of Congress Control Number: 2012944667

No portion of this book may be reproduced or transmitted in
any form, or by any means, electronic or mechanical, including
photographing, recording, or by any information and storage
retrieval system, without written permission from the publisher.

10 9 8 7 6 5 4 3 2 1

Printed and bound in China.

Contents

Introduction	4
How to Make Cake Pops	5
Fondant Fundamentals	13
Buzzing Bees	15
Three Little Piggies	23
Delicious Devil	31
Sweet Angels	39
Polly Wants a Cake Pop	47
Crazy for Cupcakes	55
Vampire's Bite	63
Cool Cat	71
Holiday Cheer	79
The Snowmen Are Coming!	87
Marshmallow Madness	95
Frankie the Monster	105
Spotty the Spider	113
Rock Star	121
Table of Equivalents	128

Introduction

E verything tastes better when it sits on a stick, or at least it's a lot more fun! It's no wonder there's a cake-pop craze sweeping the nation.

Traditional cake pops feature cake balls, a combination of cake crumbs and frosting rolled into balls and dipped in chocolate or candy coating. These bite-sized morsels are perfect for everything from a yummy treat for a child's birthday party to an elegant dessert to end a cocktail party.

Cutie Pops goes a step farther by featuring balls fashioned from not only cake, but also from brownies, cookies, marshmallows, and truffles. Included in the How to Make Cake Pops section at the start of the book are detailed instructions on how to construct the pops. The recipes that follow feature a wide variety of simple yet delectable ideas.

Cutie Pops also takes the traditional cake pop to a whole new level, transforming it into a showcase for your artistic inspiration. Following each recipe are step-by-step instructions accompanied by color photographs that show you how to fashion fondant — a sugary concoction often used to decorate wedding and other specialty cakes — into a dazzling decoration.

The recipes run the gamut from elegant to sweet, creepy to hilarious. And there's one to suit every occasion, from birthday parties to bridal or baby showers to seasonal celebrations.

So grab some lollipop sticks and get ready to have some fun!

How to Make Cake Pops

Cake pops are so much fun and also so easy to make. On the following pages are simple instructions that show you how to make cake pops. These instructions also apply to brownie and cookie pops. (The marshmallow pops have their own instructions, which you will find in Marshmallow Madness, beginning on page 95.)

The first step is to make the cake balls, which are basically a combination of crumbled cake and frosting. To make these, you will need a baked cake that has been cooled completely and some frosting (we include recipes for different cake-and-frosting combinations). When the entire cake has been crumbled, add half the frosting and mix until thoroughly combined. Gradually add more frosting until you are able to roll the mix into balls. Be careful not to add too much frosting, which would make the mix too soft.

Once you have finished rolling the cake balls, you will need to insert a lollipop stick in each one and dip each pop in melted candy coating. Candy coating usually comes with instructions, but most brands call for you to microwave the coating in a bowl for 30-second intervals at 50% power. Stir until the coating is completely melted. Candy coating is available in many different colors and can be found in craft stores such as Michaels, Hobby Lobby, and A.C. Moore, or it can be ordered online.

How to Make Cake Pops • 5

We have discovered that candy coating (see photograph below) can sometimes become too thick to effectively coat the cake balls (a high level of humidity can impact the consistency of the melted coating). If you have trouble getting it smooth and thin, do not despair. Paramount crystals — slivers of solid vegetable oil — are a handy way to thin out melted candy coating. Paramount crystals are available from specialty bake shops and can also be ordered online. Add a little bit at a time and stir until you get a fluid consistency.

Once the dipped cake pops have dried, they are ready to decorate. In addition to the recipes, the chapters that follow feature step-by-step instructions showing you how to create unique cake pops using fondant, an amazing sugary concoction that can be sculpted into many different shapes. You can find fondant at Michaels, Hobby Lobby, A.C. Moore, and other craft stores, or purchase it online. For more information on fondant, check out Fondant Fundamentals on page 13.

You will need

- Baked cake and frosting (see recipes on pages 15–93)
- Large bowl for mixing cake and frosting
- Small microwave-safe bowl for melting candy coating
- Wooden spoon for mixing
- Lollipop sticks
- Foam block (available at craft stores)
- Candy coating
- Parchment paper

Gather your materials.

Use your fingers to finely crumble the cake.

How to Make Cake Pops • 7

3.

Add frosting a little bit at a time to crumbled cake until the mix is moist enough to form cake balls. You may find that you don't need to use all the frosting. If the mix becomes too soft, the cake pops will be very difficult to dip.

4.

Use your hands to roll walnut-sized cake balls and place them on parchment paper. Refrigerate for at least 30 minutes.

5.

Create a hole in each ball by inserting a lollipop stick about halfway into the ball. Then dip the stick in melted candy coating and insert it in the hole. Allow to set for at least 15 minutes.

6.

Dip each cake pop into melted candy coating, making sure the entire ball is covered. Place the dipped cake pops in the foam block to set and dry. Once set, your pops are ready to be decorated.

Quick and Easy Decorating Tips

While *Cutie Pops* is all about creating fondant-decorated pops, we thought we would share some fun and simple ways to decorate cake pops without fondant.

You will need

- Resealable plastic bag or pastry bag
- Scissors
- Candy coating
- Edible sprinkles, glitter, or pearls
- Foam block

One easy way to decorate the pops is to drizzle melted candy coating on them using a resealable plastic bag.

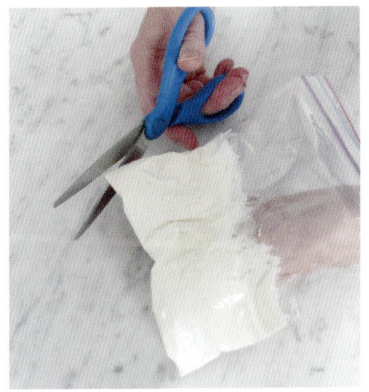

Fill a small, resealable plastic bag halfway with candy-coating wafers in the color of your choice. Make sure the bag is sealed, then place it in the microwave and melt for 30 seconds at 50% power or until the wafers are thoroughly melted. Use scissors to snip off a tiny corner of the bag.

Hold the bag as shown and gently press down to drizzle on the cake pops.

You can combine different colors and decorative techniques to create a charming display.

You can also add sprinkles or edible glitter to your dipped pops. Make sure to add these decorations before the candy coating sets.

The cake pops shown here would make a delicious Halloween treat.

Adding black drizzle and edible pearls on these white pops makes for an elegant and festive presentation, perfect for the holidays.

 # Fondant Fundamentals

A key ingredient in many wedding and other specialty cakes, fondant is a truly amazing substance. This sweet concoction was used to create all the cutie-pop decorations in this book.

We recommend that you use commercial fondant, which can be found in your local cake-supply or craft store. We suggest that you purchase white fondant and use food coloring to achieve the desired shade.

Here are some tips to follow when working with fondant:

- After adding food coloring, knead the fondant until the color is evenly blended. If you use gel food coloring (our product of choice), you may want to wear plastic gloves during this process to avoid rainbow-colored hands. (Once the food coloring is thoroughly mixed with the fondant, you won't have to worry.) It is better to make a little more of a color than you think you'll need, as it may be hard to match the color later.

- You may want to use a tiny bit of water to "glue" pieces of fondant together. For example, if you need to affix an eye to a figure and it doesn't stick properly, dip a toothpick in some water and use it to "glue" the eye on.

- When not working with the fondant, place it in a resealable plastic bag or airtight container until you are ready to use it. If stored properly at room temperature, commercial fondant will last for 18 months.

- Never put the fondant-decorated cutie pops in the refrigerator or freezer, as this will cause them to get soft and shiny. You should also avoid storing the finished pops in an airtight bag or container, as this will have a similar effect. It's important that air circulates, so that the finished fondant decorations are able to dry and harden.

Buzzing Bees
Honey Cake with Lemon Buttercream Frosting

There's no stinger in these bumbling bees buzzing in the flowers. Filled with honey cake and lemon frosting, these guys taste as sweet as they look.

Makes about 35 cake pops.

INGREDIENTS

For the Cake
- 1/2 cup light brown sugar, firmly packed
- 1 cup honey
- 1/2 cup unsalted butter, melted
- 3 eggs
- 1 teaspoon vanilla extract
- 1/2 cup milk
- 1 cup all-purpose flour
- 1 cup whole wheat flour
- 1/2 teaspoon baking soda
- 3 teaspoons baking powder
- Pinch of salt

For the Frosting
- 1 cup unsalted butter, softened
- 1 1/2 tablespoons freshly grated lemon zest
- 1 teaspoon vanilla extract
- 4 cups confectioners' sugar
- 2 teaspoons milk

For the Dipping
- 35 lollipop sticks
- 24 ounces yellow candy coating

Preheat oven to 350°F (180°C). Butter and flour a 6 X 6-inch cake pan.

For the Cake

In a medium bowl, mix together sugar, honey, butter, eggs, and vanilla until well blended. Stir in milk. In a small bowl, combine flours, baking soda, baking powder, and salt. Add the flour mix to the batter and stir gently until blended. Be careful not to overmix. Pour the batter into the prepared pan.

Bake in the center of the oven for 35 to 40 minutes or until a wooden toothpick inserted in the center of the cake comes out clean. Cool completely on a wire rack before mixing with frosting. The cake can be stored in the refrigerator in an airtight container for up to 3 days.

For the Frosting

In a large bowl, cream butter with an electric mixer on medium speed. Add lemon zest and vanilla. Gradually add sugar, beating well and scraping the sides of the bowl. Add milk and beat until light and fluffy.

Store in the refrigerator until ready to use. The frosting can be stored in a resealable container in the refrigerator for up to 2 days.

See pages 7–9 for detailed cake-pop-assembly instructions.

You will need

- Fondant in the following colors: black, white, pink
- Sharp knife
- Rolling pin

1.

Use the cake-pop mixture to roll a small tear shape.

2.

Using the technique on pages 8–9, dip the cake pop in the yellow candy coating. Let dry fully in the foam block — see step 6 on page 9 — before decorating.

Buzzing Bees • 17

3.

Use the rolling pin to flatten some black fondant. Use the sharp knife to cut 2 thin strips about 3 inches in length.

4.

Apply the strips to the bee's body as shown.

5.

With white fondant, create 2 small balls of identical size and mold them into 2 tear shapes as shown.

6.

Flatten both shapes to form wings and apply them to the bee's body as shown.

Buzzing Bees • 19

7.

With white fondant, create 2 tiny balls and flatten them.

8.

With black fondant, make teensy pupils and place them on the white fondant, and then apply the eyes to the bee as shown.

9.

With pink fondant, roll a tiny ball to create the bee's nose and apply it as shown.

10.

Roll a tiny piece of black fondant and cut it in half to form the antennas, and apply them to the bee's head as shown.

Buzzing Bees • 21

Three Little Piggies

Brownie with Milk Chocolate Ganache Frosting

These three dapper little piggies are heading to the market. Watch out for the big bad wolf, little piggies! Just like us, he can't resist your brownie and milk chocolate ganache filling.

Makes about 35 cake pops.

INGREDIENTS

For the Brownie

4 ounces unsweetened chocolate
½ cup unsalted butter
3 large eggs
1½ cups sugar
1 teaspoon vanilla extract
¾ cup all-purpose flour
Pinch of salt

For the Frosting

8 ounces milk chocolate, finely chopped
½ cup heavy cream

For the Dipping

35 lollipop sticks
24 ounces pink candy coating

Preheat oven to 350°F (180°C). Butter and flour a 7 X 7-inch cake pan.

For the Brownie

Melt chocolate and butter in a saucepan over very low heat. Mix until smooth and set aside. In a medium bowl, mix together eggs, sugar, and vanilla. Add the melted chocolate and mix well. Add flour and salt and stir, being careful not to overmix. Pour in the prepared pan.

Bake for 30 to 35 minutes or until a wooden toothpick inserted in the center comes out clean. Let cool completely before mixing with frosting. Store brownies in the refrigerator in an airtight container for up to 3 days.

For the Frosting

Put chopped chocolate in a medium-sized bowl. In a small saucepan, bring cream to a near boil. Pour the hot cream over the chocolate and stir until smooth. The frosting will thicken as it cools.

Store in the refrigerator until ready to use. The frosting can be stored in a resealable container in the refrigerator for up to 2 days.

See pages 7–9 for detailed cake-pop-assembly instructions.

You will need

- Fondant in the following colors: pink, white, black, 2 contrasting colors of choice for bow tie
- Lollipop stick
- Sharp knife
- Rolling pin

1.

Using the technique on pages 8–9, dip the cake pop in the pink candy coating. Let dry fully in the foam block — see step 6 on page 9 — before decorating.

2.

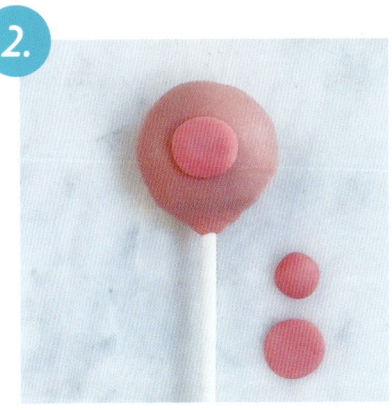

With pink fondant, roll a small ball and flatten it. Apply it to the cake pop as shown.

Three Little Piggies • 25

3.

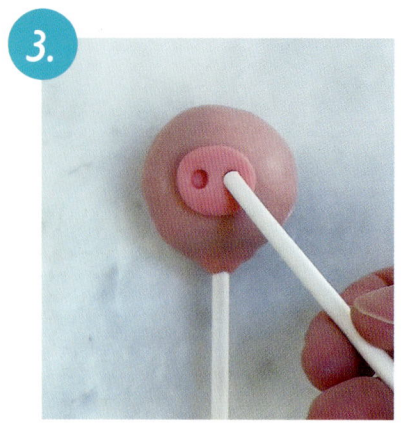

Use the lollipop stick to press 2 indentations in the pink fondant circle to make the nostrils.

4.

Flatten a small piece of pink fondant with the rolling pin and use the sharp knife to cut out 2 identical triangles.

5.

Apply the ears to the top of the pig's head as shown.

6.

Roll 2 tiny balls of white fondant for the pig's eyes.

Three Little Piggies • 27

7.

Roll 2 teensy balls of black fondant for the pupils and apply them to the white balls, and then apply them to the pig's face.

8.

Roll a small ball of pink fondant, flatten it into a circle, and cut it in half with the sharp knife.

9.

Apply a half circle over each eye to form eyelids as shown.

10.

With a color of your choice, make a small sausage shape and pinch the 2 extremities to form a bow tie. Add teensy dots with a contrasting fondant color, and place the bow tie at the base of the cake pop as shown.

Delicious Devil

Devil's Food Cake with Chocolate Buttercream Frosting

The combination of devil's food cake and chocolate buttercream frosting makes these demonic delights devilishly good. Serve them to your own little devils on Halloween or pair them with our sweet angel food cake pops on page 39.

Makes about 35 cake pops.

INGREDIENTS

For the Cake

3 ounces unsweetened chocolate
½ cup unsalted butter
2 cups packed dark brown sugar
2 large eggs
2 teaspoons vanilla extract
½ cup sour cream
2 cups all-purpose flour
2 teaspoons baking soda
Pinch of salt
1 cup boiling water

For the Frosting

1 cup unsalted butter, softened
3 cups confectioners' sugar
6 tablespoons cocoa powder
1 tablespoon milk or Grand Marnier
1 teaspoon vanilla extract

For the Dipping

35 lollipop sticks
24 ounces red candy coating

Preheat oven to 350°F (180°C). Butter and flour a 6 X 6-inch cake pan.

For the Cake

Melt chocolate and butter together in a double boiler. Place sugar in a large bowl. Stir in the melted chocolate. Add eggs and vanilla and mix until well blended. Add sour cream. In a small bowl, mix together flour, baking soda, and salt. Stir the flour mixture into the batter and stir gently until blended. Add boiling water, stir, and pour the batter into the prepared pan.

Bake for 35 minutes or until a wooden toothpick inserted in the center of the cake comes out clean. Cool completely on a wire rack before mixing with frosting. The cake can be stored in the refrigerator in an airtight container for up to 3 days.

For the Frosting

In a large bowl, cream butter with an electric mixer. Gradually add sugar and cocoa powder, beating well and scraping the sides of the bowl. Add milk and vanilla and continue beating until light and fluffy.

Store in the refrigerator until ready to use. The frosting can be stored in a resealable container in the refrigerator for up to 2 days.

See pages 7–9 for detailed cake-pop-assembly instructions.

You will need

- Fondant in the following colors: black, white, yellow
- Sharp knife

1.

Using the technique on pages 8–9, dip the cake pop in the red candy coating. Let dry fully in the foam block — see step 6 on page 9 — before decorating.

2.

With black fondant, roll 2 tiny pieces into identically shaped thin cones or horns.

Delicious Devil • 33

3.

Affix the horns on the pop as shown.

4.

Roll 2 tiny balls of white fondant and flatten them into identical circles.

5.

With yellow fondant, roll 2 even smaller identical balls, flatten them, and apply them to the white circles.

6.

With black fondant, create 2 teensy black dots for the pupils and place them on the yellow part of the eyes. Affix the eyes to the head as shown.

Delicious Devil • 35

7.

With a tiny amount of black fondant, create a very thin sausage shape, flatten it, and bend it as shown to form the eyebrows.

8.

Affix the eyebrows above the eyes as shown.

9.

With a tiny amount of black fondant, create a very thin sausage shape and flatten it to form a mouth. Place it on the face as shown.

10.

Flatten a small amount of black fondant and use the sharp knife to cut a tiny triangle for the goatee. Place it under the mouth as shown.

Delicious Devil • 37

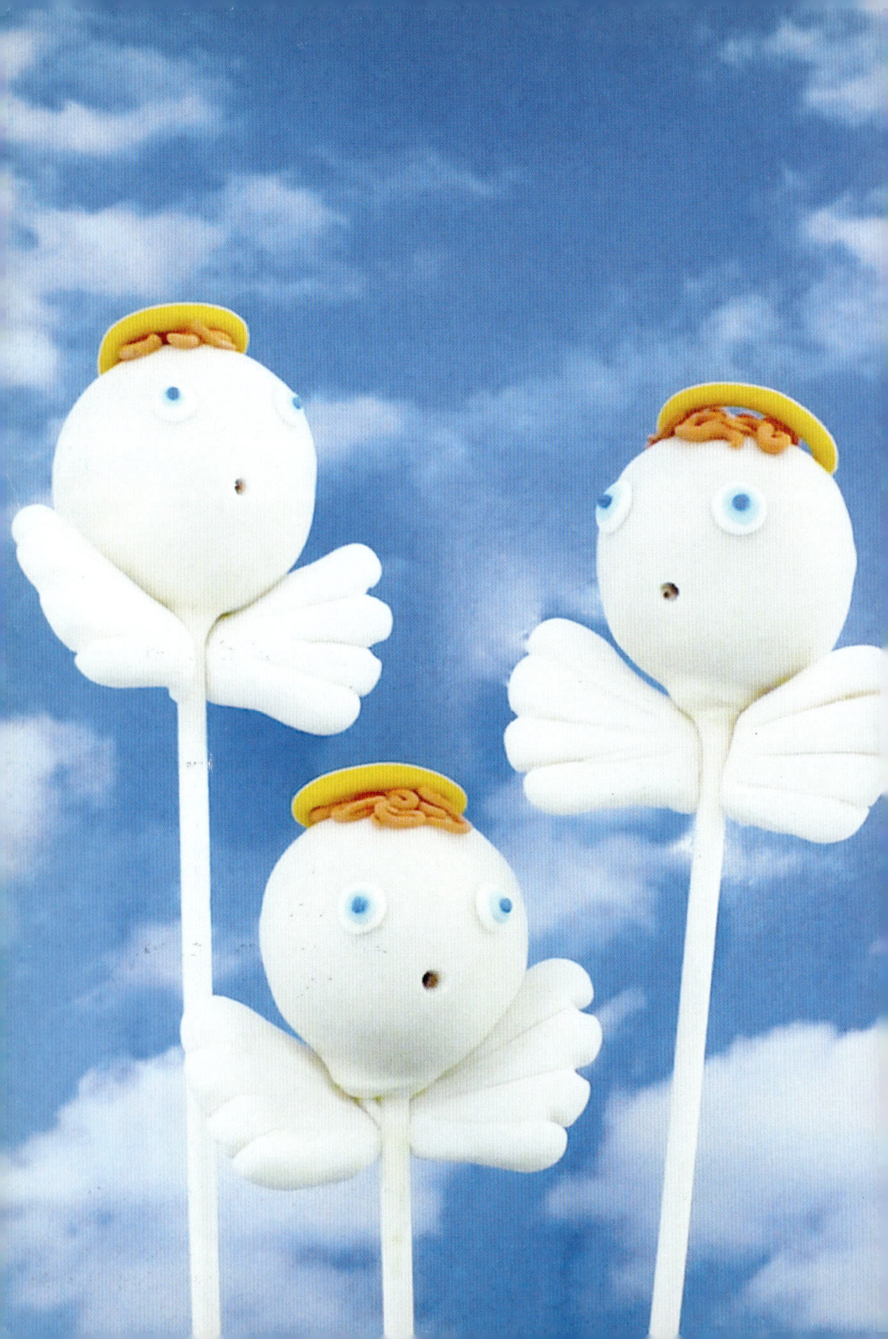

Sweet Angels
Angel's Food Cake with Vanilla Buttercream Frosting

Filled with light and airy angel food cake and creamy vanilla buttercream frosting, these sweet little angel cake pops are simply heavenly. Perfect for holiday parties, they'll leave everyone soaring through the clouds.

Makes about 35 cake pops.

INGREDIENTS

For the Cake
¾ cup confectioners' sugar
½ cup all-purpose flour
6 large egg whites
¾ teaspoon cream of tartar
¾ cup sugar
1 teaspoon vanilla extract
Pinch of salt

For the Frosting
¼ cup unsalted butter, softened
¼ teaspoon vanilla extract
1 cup confectioners' sugar
½ teaspoon milk

For the Dipping
35 lollipop sticks
24 ounces white candy coating

Preheat oven to 350°F (180°C). Use an ungreased 9 X 5-inch tube pan.

For the Cake

In a small bowl, mix together confectioners' sugar and flour. Set aside. In a large bowl, beat egg whites and cream of tartar with an electric mixer on low until frothy. Increase the beating speed to high and gradually add sugar. Then add vanilla and salt and continue to beat until stiff peaks form. It may take some time. Be patient, as it's important not to under beat. When it's ready, gently fold in the sugar/flour mixture a little at a time. Pour the batter into the ungreased tube pan. Bake for 30 minutes or until the top springs back when lightly touched. Cool on rack.

Crumble the cooled cake in a food processor until it is fine.

For the Frosting

In a large bowl, cream butter with an electric mixer. Add vanilla extract and then gradually add sugar, beating well and scraping the sides of the bowl. Add milk and beat until light and fluffy.

Store in the refrigerator until ready to use. The frosting can be stored in a resealable container in the refrigerator for up to 2 days.

See pages 7–9 for detailed cake-pop-assembly instructions.

You will need

- Fondant in the following colors: light brown, yellow, white, light blue, dark blue
- Toothpick
- Sharp knife

1.

Using the technique on pages 8–9, dip the cake pop in the white candy coating. Let dry fully in the foam block — see step 6 on page 9 — before decorating.

2.

With light-brown fondant, roll a tiny piece into a very thin strand and scrunch it up as shown, and place it immediately on the angel's head.

Sweet Angels • 41

3.

Repeat the previous step 4 times until you have a small patch of hair on top of the angel's head.

4.

With yellow fondant, roll a small, thin strip of about 2½ inches in length.

5.

Attach the 2 ends together to form a circle and place the resulting halo on the head as shown.

6.

For the eyes, roll 2 small balls of white fondant and flatten them into identical circles. With light-blue fondant, roll 2 even smaller identical balls, flatten them, and apply them to the white circles. Place them on the angel's face as shown.

Sweet Angels • 43

7.

With dark-blue fondant, create 2 teensy dots for the pupils and place them on the light-blue part of the eyes.

8.

With the toothpick, make a small hole for the angel's mouth as shown.

9.

With white fondant, form a triangle as shown. With the sharp knife, create 3 indentations. Use the toothpick to gently shape the edge of the wing as shown.

10.

Repeat the step above to make a second wing. Apply the 2 wings below the angel's head as shown. You may have to prop up the angel so that its head rests on its wings until they are fully dry (it may take a day or so).

Sweet Angels • 45

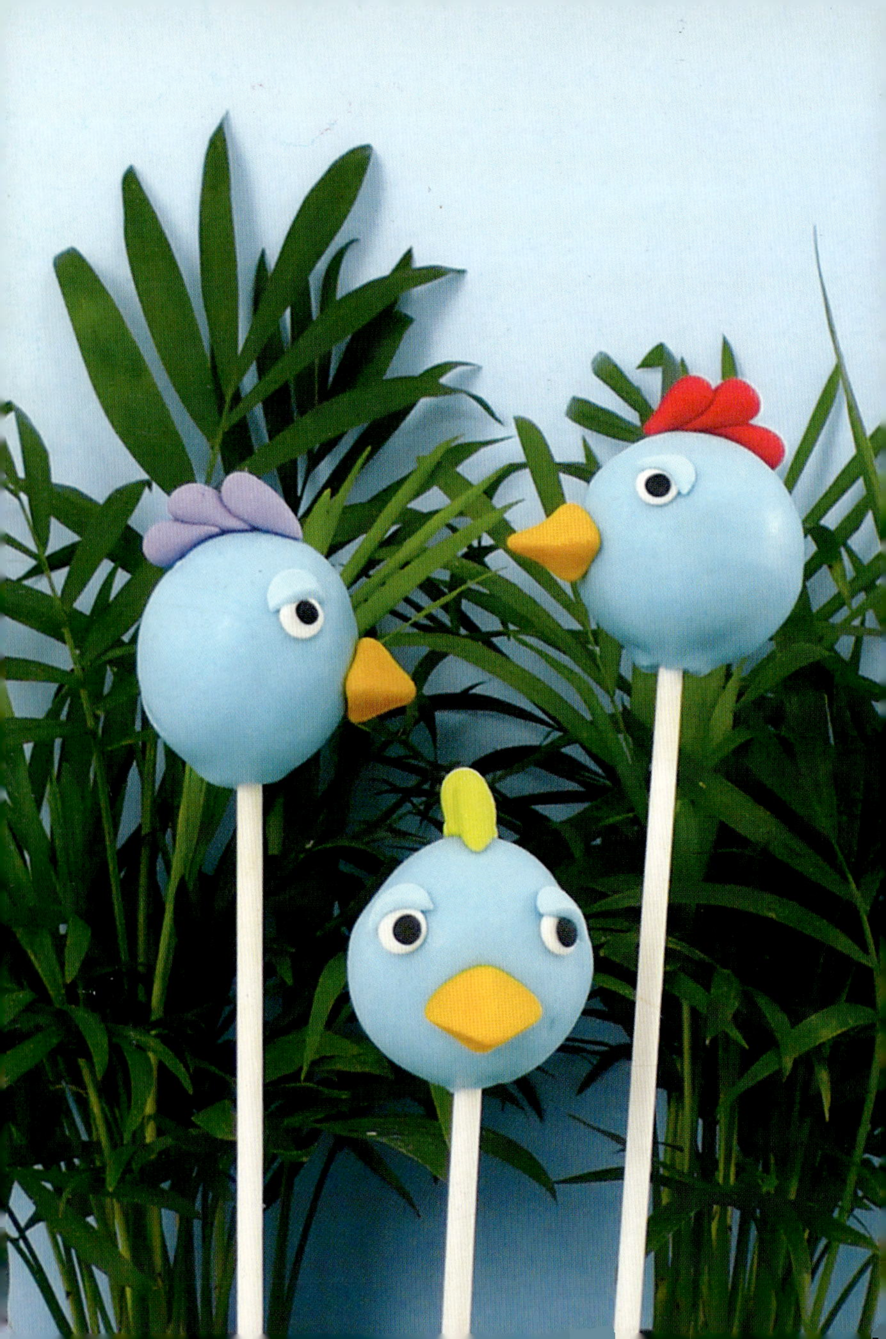

Polly Wants a Cake Pop

Yellow Cake with Lime Buttercream Frosting

These tropical birds of a feather are flocking together in their jungle retreat. Filled with yellow cake and lime buttercream frosting, they are in fine feather. Such a refreshing combination!

Makes about 35 cake pops.

INGREDIENTS

For the Cake

1 1/4 cups all-purpose flour
1/2 teaspoon baking soda
1 teaspoon baking powder
Pinch of salt
1/2 cup unsalted butter, softened
1 cup sugar
3 large eggs, separated
1 teaspoon vanilla extract
1/2 cup sour cream

For the Frosting

1 cup unsalted butter, softened
1 1/2 tablespoons freshly grated lime zest
2 teaspoons lime juice
4 cups confectioners' sugar
1 tablespoon milk

For the Dipping

35 lollipop sticks
24 ounces blue candy coating

Preheat oven to 350°F (180°C). Butter and flour an 8 X 8-inch cake pan.

For the Cake

In a medium bowl, mix together flour, baking soda, baking powder, and salt. Set aside. In a larger bowl, cream butter and sugar together until light and fluffy. Add egg yolks one at a time, reserving the whites in a separate bowl. Mix well after each addition, and then add vanilla. Add the flour mix, alternately with the sour cream. Beat egg whites with an electric mixer on high speed until stiff, and then gently fold into the rest of the batter with a wooden spoon. Pour the batter into the prepared pan.

Bake for 35 minutes or until a wooden toothpick inserted in the center of the cake comes out clean. Cool completely on a wire rack before mixing with frosting. The cake can be stored in the refrigerator in an airtight container for up to 3 days.

For the Frosting

In a large bowl, cream butter with an electric mixer on medium speed. Add lime zest and juice. Gradually add sugar, beating well and scraping the sides of the bowl. Add milk and continue beating until light and fluffy.

Store in the refrigerator until ready to use. The frosting can be stored in a resealable container in the refrigerator for up to 2 days.

See pages 7–9 for detailed cake-pop-assembly instructions.

You will need

- **Fondant in the following colors: green, yellow, white, black, blue**
- **Sharp knife**

1.

Using the technique on pages 8–9, dip the cake pop in the blue candy coating. Let dry fully in the foam block — see step 6 on page 9 — before decorating.

2.

With green fondant, roll a tear shape as shown.

Polly Wants a Cake Pop • 49

3.

Create 2 more identical tear shapes. Bring the tear shapes together to form the bird's plume as shown.

4.

Place the plume on top of the head.

5.

With a small amount of yellow fondant, roll a ball and shape it into a cone. Press the base of the cone on a flat surface, positioning your fingers as shown to create a 4-sided pyramid. This will be the beak.

6.

Apply the beak to the head.

Polly Wants a Cake Pop • 51

7.

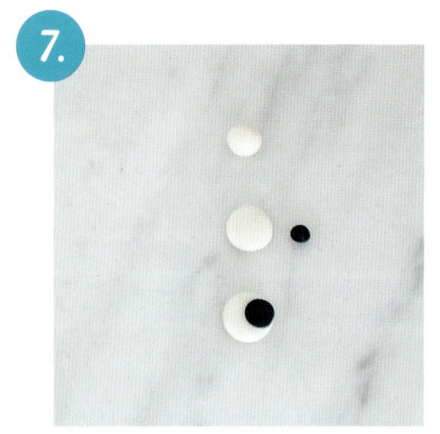

With white fondant, create 2 small balls and flatten them to create the eyes. Add a tiny dot of black fondant and flatten slightly to form the pupils.

8.

Apply the eyes to the head as shown.

52 • CUTIE POPS

9.

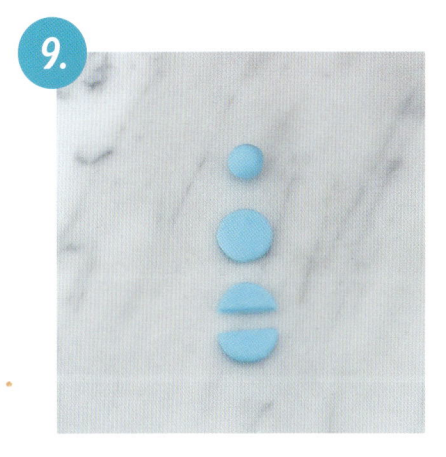

With blue fondant, roll a small ball, flatten it, and cut it in half with the sharp knife to form the eyelids.

10.

Apply the eyelids to the face as shown.

Polly Wants a Cake Pop • 53

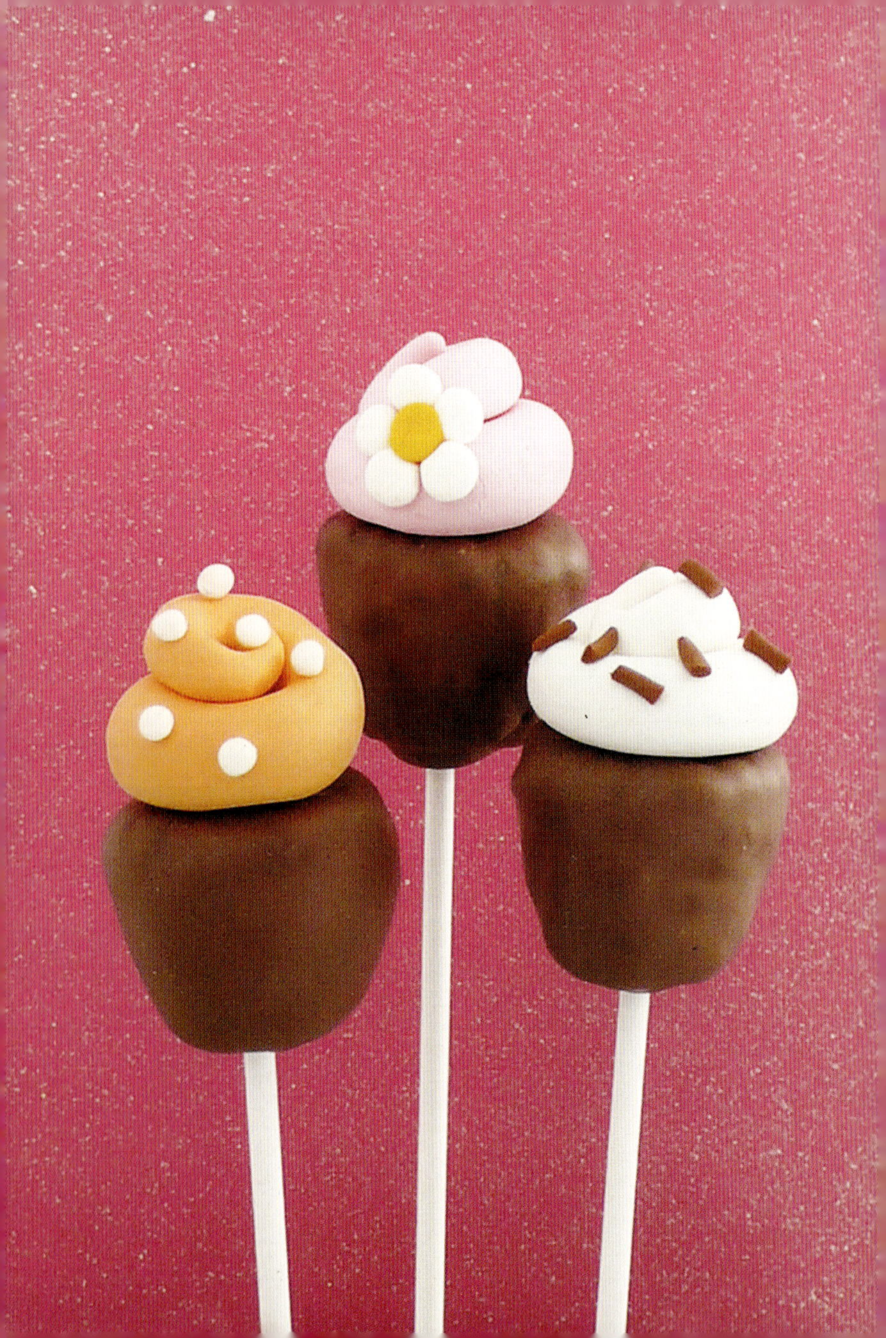

Crazy for Cupcakes
Pumpkin Cake with Cardamom Cream Cheese Frosting

Cupcakes are nice, but cupcake cutie pops are just plain irresistible. The ones shown here are composed of pumpkin cake and cardamom cream cheese frosting, but feel free to choose your favorite cake-frosting combination. Accessorize with flowers, sprinkles, or pearls. Too cute!

Makes about 35 cake pops.

INGREDIENTS

For the Cake
1 cup all-purpose flour
1/2 teaspoon baking soda
1 teaspoon baking powder
Pinch of salt
1 cup sugar
1 teaspoon cinnamon
1/4 teaspoon freshly grated nutmeg
1/8 teaspoon ground cloves
1 cup solid canned pumpkin (not pumpkin filling)
2 large eggs
1/4 cup vegetable oil
1 teaspoon vanilla extract

For the Frosting
1 8-ounce package cream cheese, softened
1/4 cup unsalted butter, softened
1 1/4 cups confectioners' sugar
1 teaspoon cardamom powder

For the Dipping
35 lollipop sticks
24 ounces light cocoa candy coating

Preheat oven to 350°F (180°C). Butter and flour an 8 X 8-inch cake pan.

For the Cake

In a large bowl, mix together flour, baking soda, baking powder, salt, sugar, cinnamon, nutmeg, and cloves. Set aside. In a medium bowl, mix together pumpkin, eggs, oil, and vanilla. Add the pumpkin mixture to the flour mixture and stir with a wooden spoon. Do not overmix.

Pour the batter into the prepared pan. Bake for 35 minutes or until a wooden toothpick inserted in the center of the cake comes out clean. Cool completely on a wire rack before mixing with frosting. The cake can be stored in the refrigerator in an airtight container for up to 3 days.

For the Frosting

Beat together cream cheese and butter with an electric mixer on medium speed. Gradually beat in sugar and continue mixing until smooth. Blend in cardamom powder.

Store in the refrigerator until ready to use. The frosting can be stored in a resealable container in the refrigerator for up to 2 days.

See pages 7–9 for detailed cake-pop-assembly instructions.

You will need

- Fondant in the following colors: pink, white, yellow, brown
- Sharp knife

1.

Using the technique on pages 8–9, dip the cake pop in the light cocoa candy coating. Let dry fully in the foam block — see step 6 on page 9 — before decorating.

2.

With pink fondant, roll a long sausage shape (around 3 inches in length) and make one end thinner as shown.

Crazy for Cupcakes • 57

3.

Roll the pink sausage onto itself as shown to form the frosting.

4.

Place the frosting on top of the cupcake.

5.

To make a decorative flower, roll 5 identical small white balls.

6.

Flatten the balls slightly and arrange them in a circle.

Crazy for Cupcakes • 59

7.

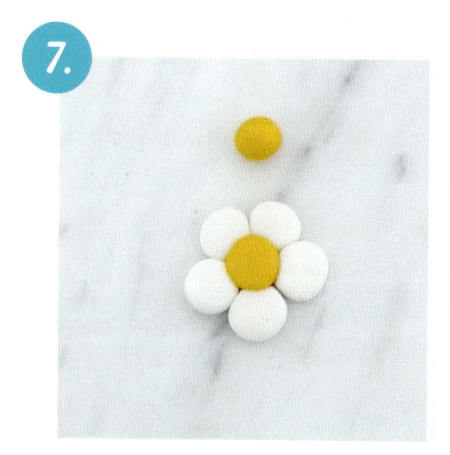

Roll a small ball of yellow fondant, place it in the center of the flower, and press lightly.

8.

Place the flower on the cupcake.

9.

To make sprinkles, roll a very thin sausage shape out of brown fondant and use the sharp knife to cut it in tiny strips. Place them randomly around the frosting as shown.

10.

To make decorative pearls, roll tiny balls of white fondant and place them randomly around the frosting as shown.

Crazy for Cupcakes • 61

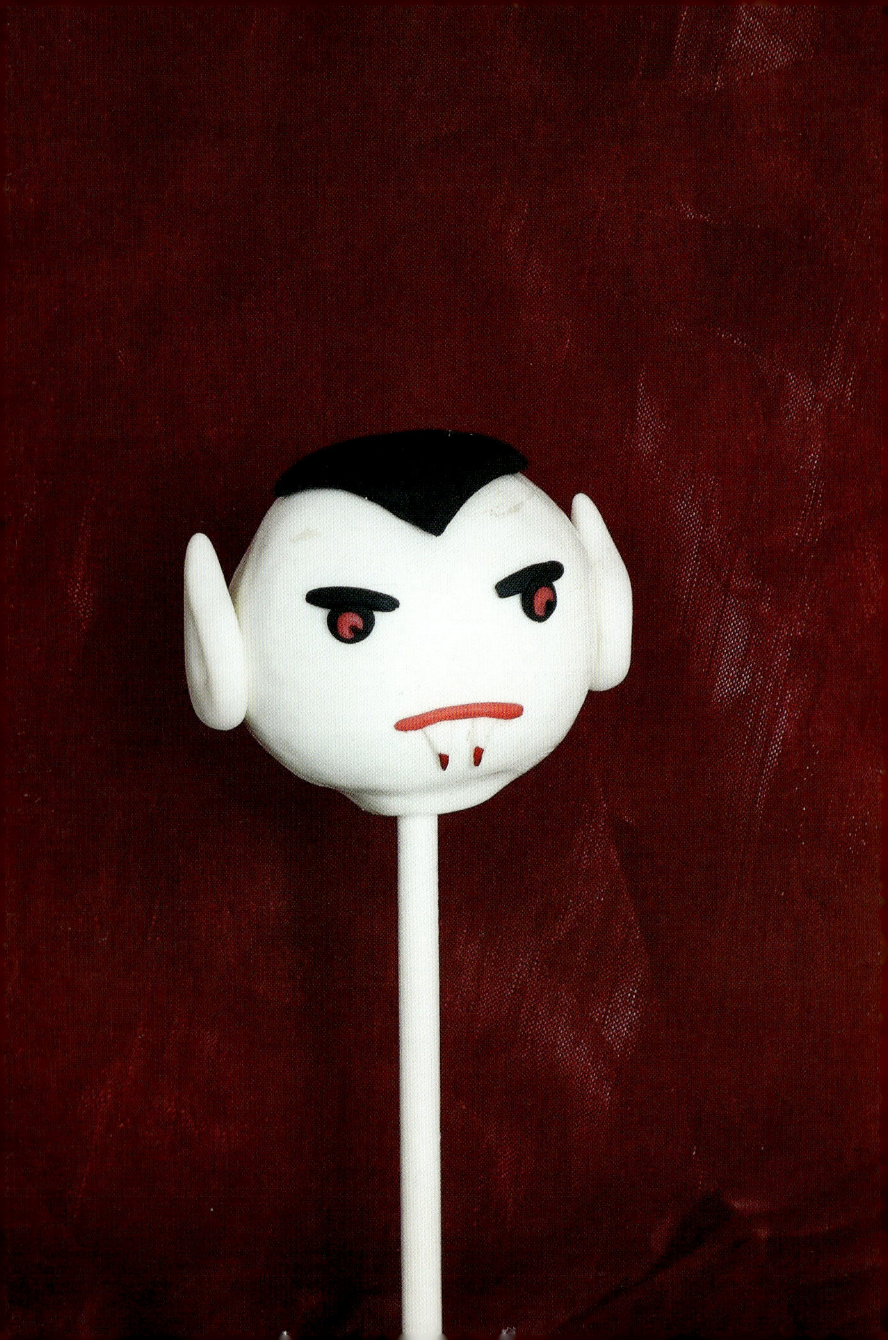

Vampire's Bite

Red Velvet Cake with Cream Cheese Frosting

This mesmerizing vampire is surprisingly sweet. Hidden beneath his ghostly pale exterior is an exquisite red velvet cake pop. To increase his intensity, we added small red dots to his pupils. No one can resist the count.

Makes about 35 cake pops.

INGREDIENTS

For the Cake
1 ¼ cups all-purpose flour
¼ cup unsweetened cocoa powder
1 teaspoon baking soda
Pinch of salt
½ cup unsalted butter, softened
1 cup sugar
2 large eggs
½ cup sour cream
¼ cup milk
1 teaspoon vanilla extract
1 teaspoon red food coloring (or more as needed)

For the Frosting
1 8-ounce package cream cheese, softened
¼ cup unsalted butter, softened
1 ¼ cups confectioners' sugar

For the Dipping
35 lollipop sticks
24 ounces white candy coating

Preheat oven to 350°F (180°C). Butter and flour an 8 X 8-inch cake pan.

For the Cake

In a medium bowl, mix together flour, cocoa powder, baking soda, and salt. Set aside. In a large bowl, beat butter and sugar together with an electric mixer on medium speed until light and fluffy. Beat in eggs one at a time. Add sour cream, milk, vanilla, and red food coloring, and mix well. Gradually add the flour mixture to the batter and stir gently until blended. Pour the batter into the prepared pan.

Bake for 35 minutes or until a wooden toothpick inserted in the center of the cake comes out clean. Cool completely on a wire rack before mixing with frosting. The cake can be stored in the refrigerator in an airtight container for up to 3 days.

For the Frosting

In a large bowl, beat together cream cheese and butter with an electric mixer on medium speed until smooth. Gradually beat in sugar and continue beating until light and fluffy.

Store in the refrigerator until ready to use. The frosting can be stored in a resealable container in the refrigerator for up to 2 days.

See pages 7–9 for detailed cake-pop-assembly instructions.

You will need

- Fondant in the following colors: black, red, white
- Toothpick
- Red food coloring
- Rolling pin

1.

Using the technique on pages 8–9, dip the cake pop in the white candy coating. Let dry fully in the foam block — see step 6 on page 9 — before decorating.

2.

Roll out a small amount of black fondant and use the sharp knife to cut out a small triangle.

Vampire's Bite • 65

3.

Apply the triangle to the top of the vampire's head.

4.

With black fondant, roll 2 tiny strips. Roll 2 tiny balls of black fondant, flatten them, and apply them below the strips as shown to form the vampire's eyes.

5.

Apply the eyes to the face as shown.

6.

With red fondant, roll a very thin line to create the mouth and apply it to the face.

Vampire's Bite • 67

7.

Roll out a small amount of white fondant and use the sharp knife to cut 2 tiny triangles to form the teeth. Apply them to the mouth as shown.

8.

Dip the toothpick in red food coloring and apply it to the bottom of each tooth.

9.

With a small amount of white fondant, make 2 identical cone shapes and flatten them to form the vampire's ears.

10.

Apply the ears to the sides of the head, shape them, and create holes in each with the toothpick.

Vampire's Bite • 69

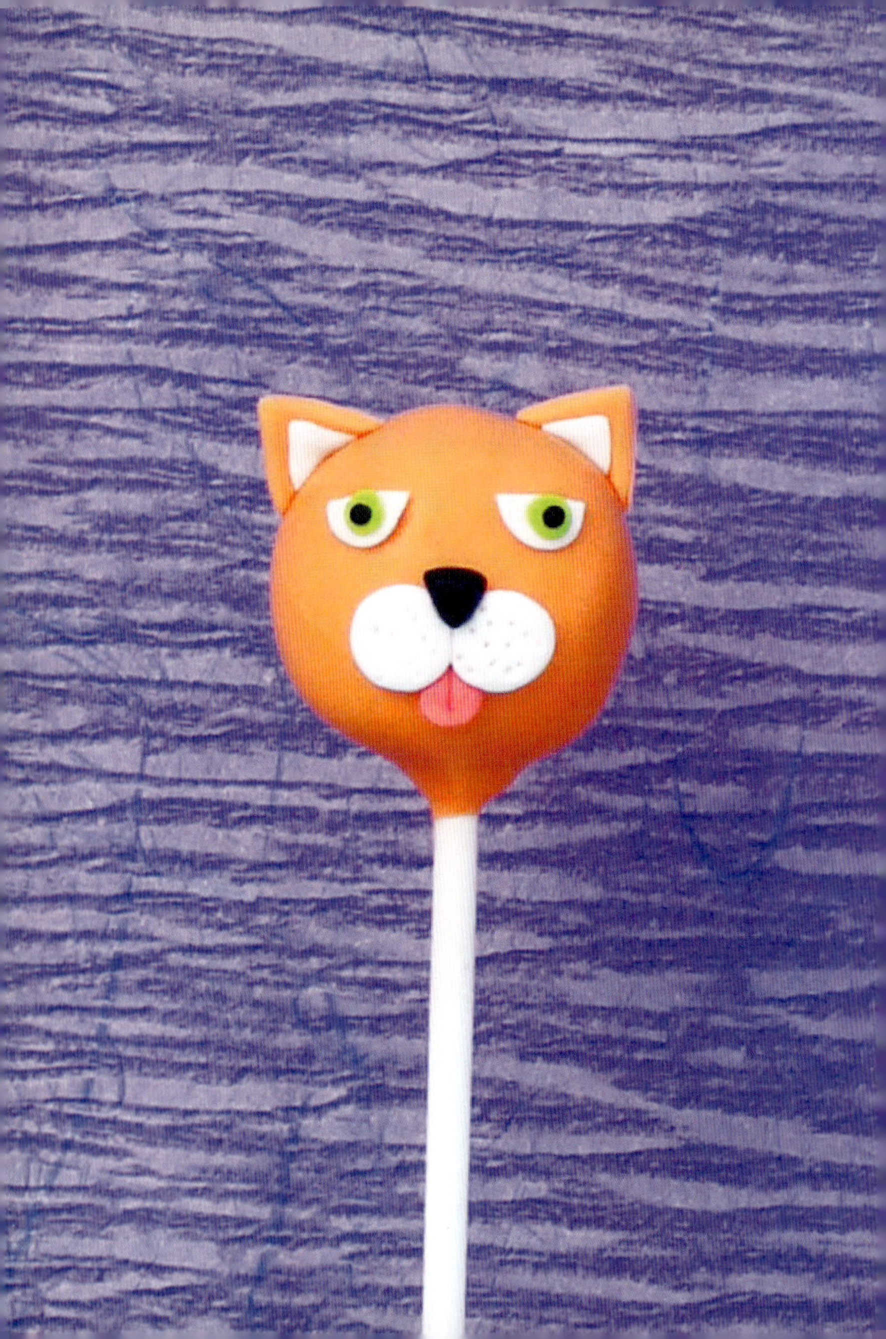

Cool Cat

Chocolate Cookies with White Chocolate Ganache

Cookies and cream are the secret to this cool tabby cat's heart. Filled with crumbly chocolate cookies combined with white chocolate ganache, these cutie pops are the cat's meow.

Makes about 35 cake pops.

INGREDIENTS

For the Cookies

1/2 cup all-purpose flour
1/4 cup unsweetened cocoa powder
1/2 cup confectioners' sugar
Pinch of salt
1/8 teaspoon baking soda
1/2 cup unsalted butter, cold and cut into small pieces
1 teaspoon vanilla extract
1 tablespoon milk

For the Ganache

16 ounces white chocolate, finely chopped
4 tablespoons heavy cream

For the Dipping

35 lollipop sticks
24 ounces orange candy coating

Preheat oven to 350°F (180°C). Butter 2 cookie sheets.

For the Cookies

In a food processor, mix together flour, cocoa powder, sugar, salt, and baking soda. Add butter, vanilla, and milk, and pulse a few times until the dough comes together. Transfer the dough to a bowl and make sure it is well mixed. Shape it into a small log about 8 inches long and wrap it in plastic wrap. Place the log in the refrigerator for at least 1 hour. When you are ready to bake the cookies, unwrap the log and slice it thinly (about ⅛ of an inch). Place the cookies on the cookie sheets as you slice them.

Bake the cookies for 12 to 14 minutes. Cool on the cookie sheets. The cookies will be very crumbly, ready to mix with the white chocolate ganache to create the cookies-and-cream mixture.

For the Ganache

Place chopped chocolate and cream in a double boiler over a medium flame and carefully stir until the chocolate is melted and the mixture is smooth. While the ganache is still warm, add the crumbled cookies and mix together. Let set before forming into balls.

See pages 7–9 for detailed cake-pop-assembly instructions.

You will need

- Fondant in the following colors: white, pink, black, green, orange
- Toothpick
- Sharp knife
- Rolling pin

1.

Using the technique on pages 8–9, dip the cake pop in the orange candy coating. Let dry fully in the foam block — see step 6 on page 9 — before decorating.

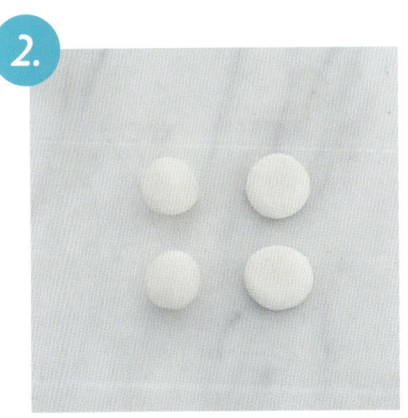

2.

With white fondant, roll 2 small balls and flatten them slightly.

Cool Cat • 73

3.

Apply the flattened balls to the pop, side by side as shown. With a toothpick, make little holes in the white balls.

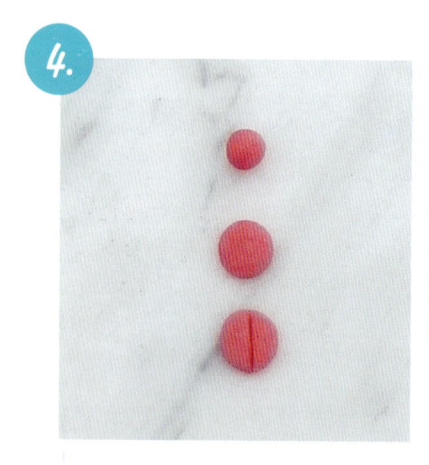

4.

Roll a tiny amount of pink fondant into a ball and flatten it. With the sharp knife, make an indentation in the center.

5.

Apply the tongue to the cat's face as shown.

6.

Use black fondant to make a tiny triangle. Apply it to the cat's face as shown.

Cool Cat • 75

7.

To create the eyes, use white fondant to make a small ball, flatten it, and cut it in half with the knife. With a tiny amount of green fondant, make 2 identical balls, flatten them, and apply them to the white halves. Add 2 teensy black dots for the pupils.

8.

Apply the eyes to the cat's face.

9.

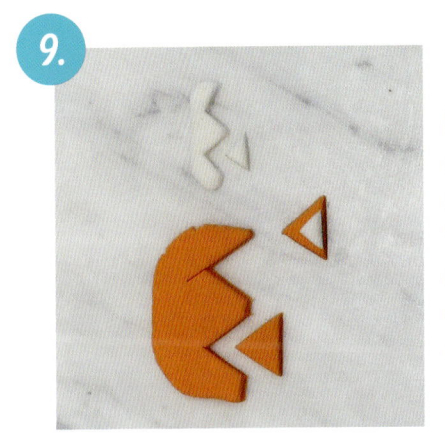

Roll out a small amount of orange fondant. Use the knife to cut triangles. With white fondant, make 2 tiny triangles and apply them to the orange ears as shown.

10.

Apply the ears to the cat's face and shape them as shown.

Cool Cat • 77

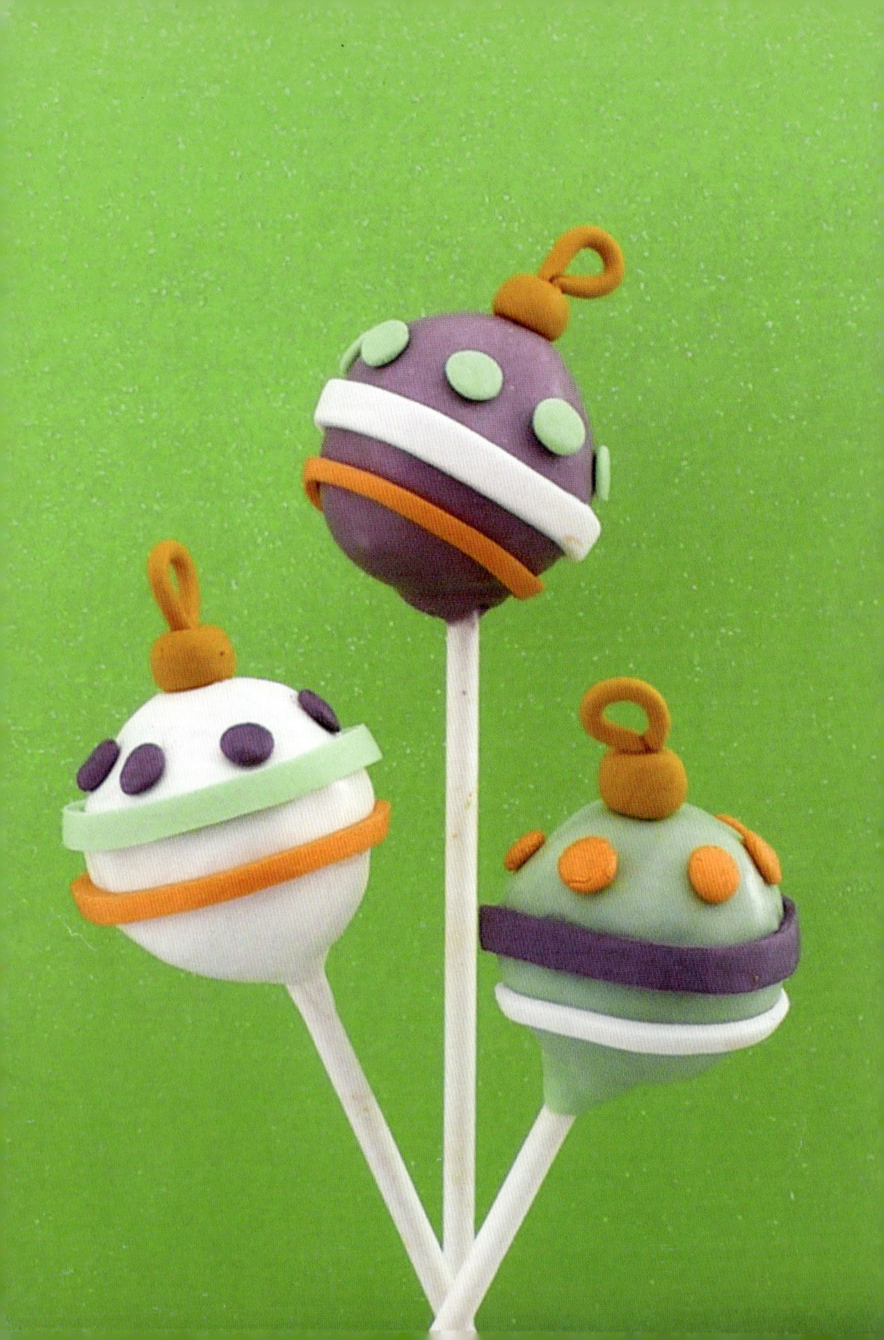

Holiday Cheer
Dark Chocolate Truffles

Decorate your holiday table with these elegant dark chocolate truffle ornaments. For a more sophisticated flavor, substitute rum or whiskey for the vanilla extract. These little truffle pops will vanish before your eyes.

Makes about 30 truffle pops.

INGREDIENTS

For the Truffles

16 ounces dark semisweet chocolate, finely chopped
1 cup heavy cream
1 teaspoon vanilla extract

For the Dipping

30 lollipop sticks
8 ounces lavender candy coating, 8 ounces white candy coating, and 8 ounces green candy coating

Place chopped chocolate in a medium bowl. Place cream in a saucepan and heat over a medium flame until it is just simmering. Remove the cream from the heat and pour it over the chocolate, making sure that all the chocolate is covered. Let it sit for a minute or so, and then gently stir until it is smooth. When the mixture is smooth, add vanilla and stir until it is fully incorporated.

Let the ganache cool at room temperature for 30 minutes. Cover the top of the ganache with plastic wrap or parchment paper cut to fit (the wrap or parchment paper should sit gently on top of the ganache). Place the bowl in the refrigerator until it is firm (for about 2 hours).

When it is set, scoop out a little more than a teaspoon of the ganache and roll it between the palms of your hands to form a ¾-inch or walnut-sized ball. The truffles don't have to look perfect at this point. Place the balls on parchment paper and return them to the refrigerator for about an hour more. Roll the ganache between your palms again, smoothing out any lumps, until all the balls are smooth and round.

These truffles can be stored at room temperature for up to 4 days or in the refrigerator for up to a week.

See pages 7–9 for detailed cake-pop-assembly instructions.

You will need

- Fondant in the following colors: gold, white, orange, pale green
- Toothpick
- Sharp knife
- Rolling pin

1.

Using the technique on pages 8–9, dip the cake pop in the lavender candy coating. Let dry fully in the foam block — see step 6 on page 9 — before decorating.

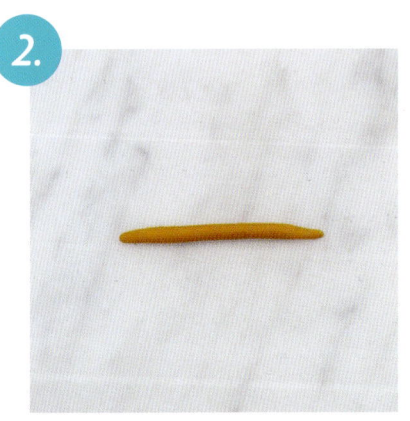

2.

With gold fondant, roll a very thin strip about an inch in length.

Holiday Cheer • 81

3.

Fold the strip in half to form a loop.

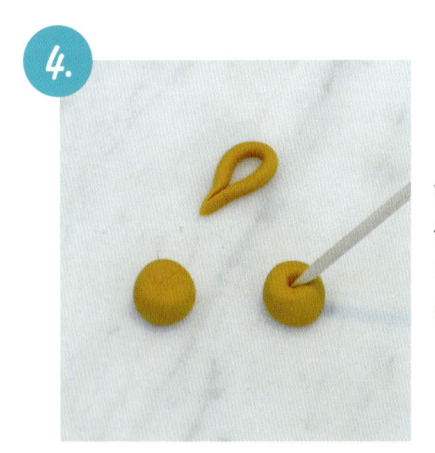

4.

With the same color fondant, roll a tiny cylinder. Use the toothpick to make a hole at the top.

5.

Insert the end of the loop into the hole as shown.

6.

Place it on the top of the pop at a slight angle.

Holiday Cheer • 83

7.

Roll out a piece of white fondant, and use the sharp knife to cut a thin strip long enough to wrap around the ball.

8.

Wrap the strip around the pop as shown.

9.

Repeat step 7, using orange fondant to create a thinner strip. Wrap the orange strip below the white one.

10.

With pale-green fondant, make tiny balls and flatten them to create dots. Apply them to the ornament as shown.

Holiday Cheer • 85

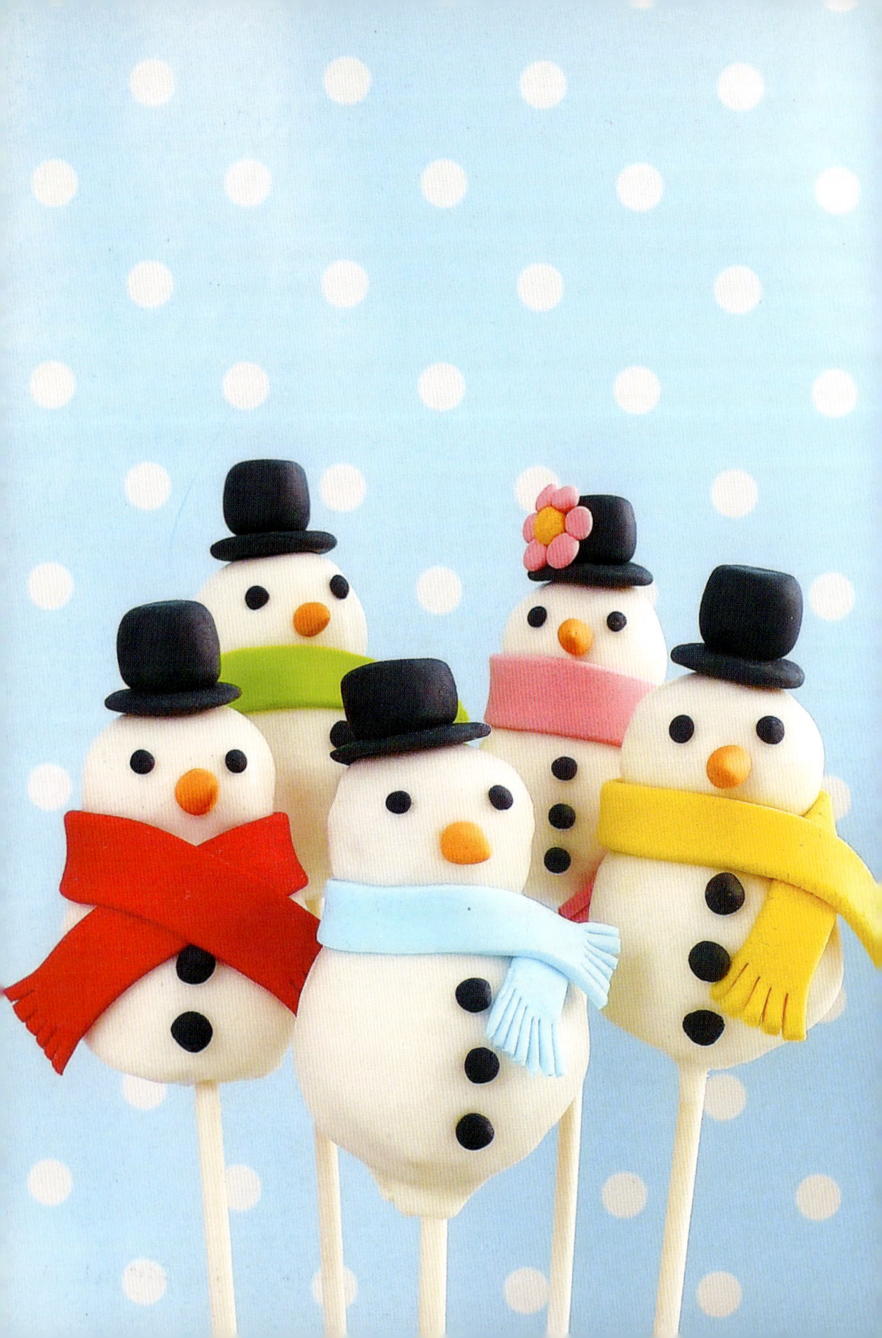

The Snowmen Are Coming!

White Cake with Vanilla Buttercream Frosting

Imagine opening your door to this band of merry carolers. With their coal-black eyes, carrot noses, and fashionable accessories, they are a welcome addition to any party.

Makes about 25 cake pops.

INGREDIENTS

For the Cake

1 cup sugar
1/2 cup unsalted butter, softened
1 1/4 cups all-purpose flour
Pinch of salt
2 teaspoons baking powder
1/2 teaspoon baking soda
1/4 cup milk
1/4 cup sour cream
3 large egg whites
2 teaspoons vanilla extract

For the Frosting

1 cup unsalted butter, softened
1 teaspoon vanilla extract
4 cups confectioners' sugar
2 teaspoons milk

For the Dipping

25 lollipop sticks
24 ounces white candy coating

Preheat oven to 350°F (180°C). Butter and flour a 6 X 6-inch cake pan.

For the Cake

In a large bowl, cream sugar and butter. In a medium bowl, combine flour, salt, baking powder, and baking soda. In another medium bowl, whisk together milk, sour cream, egg whites, and vanilla. Alternate adding the milk mixture and flour mixture to the butter mixture. Be careful not to overmix. Pour the batter into the prepared pan.

Bake for 35 to 40 minutes or until a toothpick inserted in the center of the cake comes out clean. Cool completely on a wire rack before mixing with frosting. The cake can be stored in the refrigerator in an airtight container for up to 3 days.

For the Frosting

In a large bowl, cream butter with an electric mixer on medium speed. Add vanilla and then gradually add sugar, beating well and scraping the sides of the bowl. Add milk and beat until light and fluffy. Store in the refrigerator until ready to use. The frosting can be stored in a resealable container in the refrigerator for up to 2 days.

See pages 7–9 for detailed cake-pop-assembly instructions.

You will need:

- Fondant in the following colors: black, orange, color of choice for scarf
- Sharp knife
- Toothpick

1. For each snowman, roll 2 cake balls: a small one for the head and a larger one for the body. Press them together. Using the technique on pages 8–9, dip the cake pop in the white candy coating. Let dry fully in the foam block — see step 6 on page 9 — before decorating.

2. With black fondant, shape 2 tiny balls for the snowman's eyes and apply them to the head as shown.

The Snowmen Are Coming! • 89

3.

With a small amount of orange fondant, create a carrot-shaped nose and apply it as shown.

4.

With black fondant, make 3 tiny balls for the coal buttons and apply them as shown.

5.

Take a small amount of black fondant, roll it into a ball, and flatten it into a thin circle.

6.

Using a little more black fondant than in step 5, create a cylinder shape and apply it to the top of the circle to form a hat.

The Snowmen Are Coming! • 91

7.

Place the hat on the snowman's head.

8.

Choose whatever fondant color you like to make the snowman's scarf. Make a thin sausage shape and flatten it as shown.

9.

With the sharp knife or toothpick, make indentations on both ends of the scarf to form a fringe.

10.

Carefully wrap the scarf around the snowman's neck.

The Snowmen Are Coming! • 93

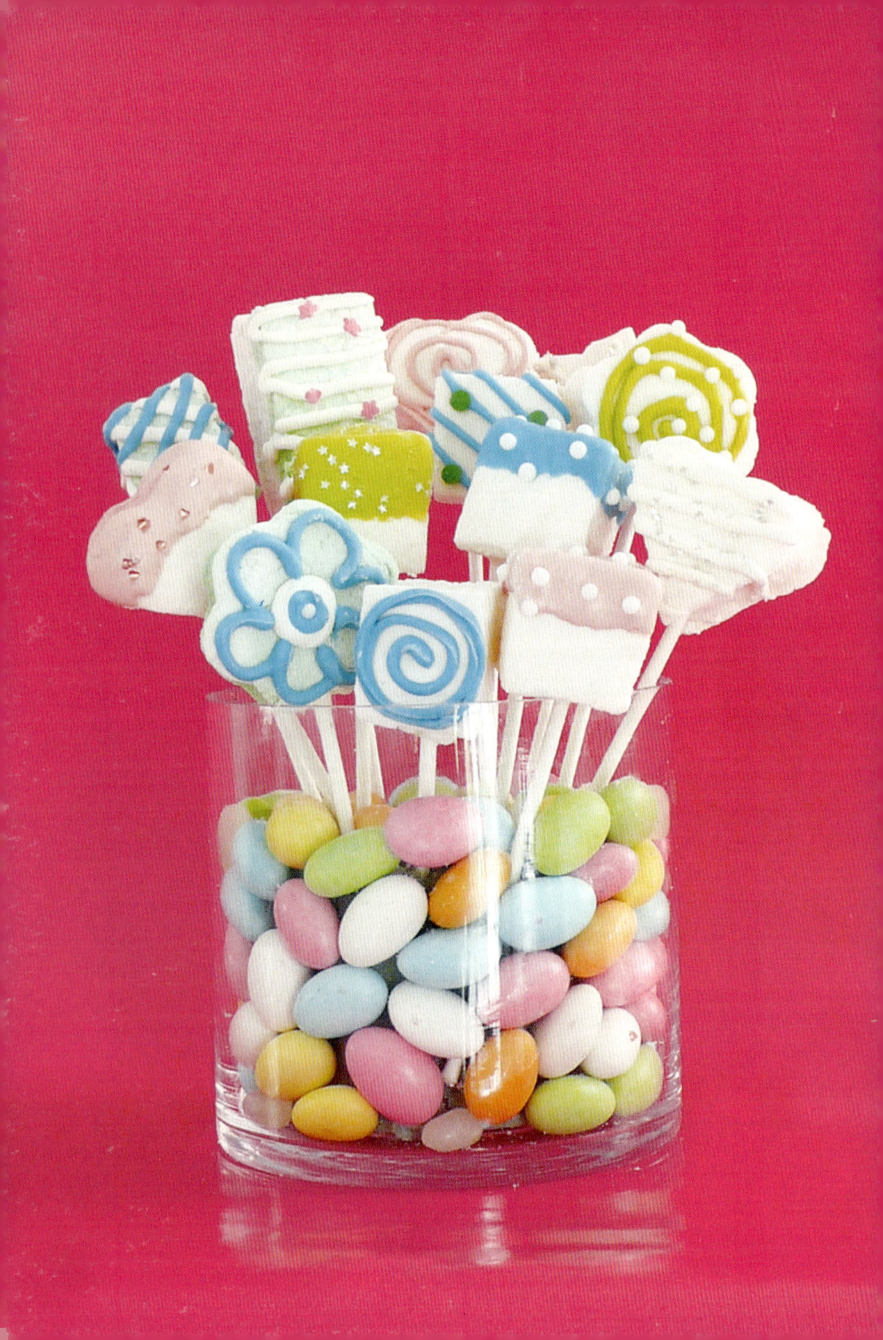

Marshmallow Madness

Classic Vanilla Marshmallows

Nothing says fun like marshmallows! These soft puffy clouds are delicious on their own, but they are even more sublime when dipped in chocolate or candy coating.

Since marshmallows are a little more complicated to make than the other cutie pops, we have included step-by-step instructions. Like all cutie pops, they come in many different shapes, flavors, and colors and can be decorated in many fun ways.

Makes about 35 marshmallow pops.

INGREDIENTS

For the Marshmallows

1/2 cup confectioners' sugar
1/2 cup cornstarch
1/2 cup cold water, plus 1/3 cup
3 1/4-ounce packages unflavored gelatin
2 cups sugar
2/3 cup light corn syrup
2 large egg whites, at room temperature
1/4 teaspoon salt
2 teaspoons vanilla extract
Food coloring of your choice (optional)

For the Assembly

35 lollipop sticks
8 ounces white candy coating
9 X 9-inch cake pan
Foam block

For the Decoration

Candy coating in an array of colors
Edible glitter
Edible sprinkles
Edible pearls

1. In a small bowl, mix together confectioners' sugar and cornstarch with a spoon, then sprinkle enough of the mixture to cover the bottom of the cake pan and set aside. Reserve the remaining mixture for later. You will also need an electric mixer, candy thermometer, a 2-quart saucepan, a wooden spoon, and a small and large bowl, a sieve, a cutting board, a sharp knife, and (optional) cookie cutters.

2. Place ½ cup cold water in the small bowl. Sprinkle gelatin powder on top and gently stir. Set aside.

3.

In a medium saucepan, mix together sugar, corn syrup, and the remaining 1/3 cup of cold water. Bring to a boil and continue cooking over medium-high heat.

4.

Meanwhile, place egg whites in the large bowl, add salt, and use the mixer on high speed to whip the egg whites until soft peaks form.

Marshmallow Madness • 97

5.

Using the candy thermometer, watch until it reaches 245°F (118°C), then quickly stir the gelatin mixture into the sugar mixture, and mix until it is completely incorporated.

6.

With the mixer on low speed, slowly pour the hot gelatin-and-sugar mixture into the beaten egg whites.

7. Increase the speed to high and continue to whip on high speed until the mixture thickens and doubles in size (for about 12 minutes with a handheld mixer and 6 minutes with a standing mixer). Add the vanilla and mix well. (You can substitute peppermint or almond extract or another flavoring if you like. This is also a good time to add any food coloring.)

8. Pour the marshmallow mixture into the prepared cake pan. Use the sieve to dust the top thoroughly with some of the reserved confectioners'-sugar-and-cornstarch mix. Allow to stand uncovered at room temperature for at least 4 hours, preferably overnight.

Marshmallow Madness • 99

9.

When the marshmallow has set, turn it over onto the cutting board. Dust the bottom with more of the confectioners'-sugar-and-cornstarch mix.

10.

Use the sharp knife to cut the marshmallow into squares. You can also use a pizza cutter.

11.

And you have a trove of delicious homemade marshmallows! They look lovely in their traditional square shape.

12.

You can also use cookie cutters to make different shapes.

Marshmallow Madness • 101

13.

To make a pop, use a lollipop stick to make a hole. Dip the stick in the melted white candy coating, insert it in the prepared hole, and allow it to dry.

14.

These fun shapes are perfect for a child's birthday party. We added a little red food coloring to the marshmallow mixture to make the heart marshmallows pink (see step 7 on page 99).

15.

Use the drizzling techniques found on page 11 to decorate the marshmallow pops. The pop on the left is an example of a pink-colored marshmallow layered over green-colored marshmallow and allowed to set in the same pan.

16.

You can also dip the marshmallow tops in melted chocolate or colorful candy coating and decorate them with edible pearls, sprinkles, and glitter. There are many creative possibilities.

Marshmallow Madness • 103

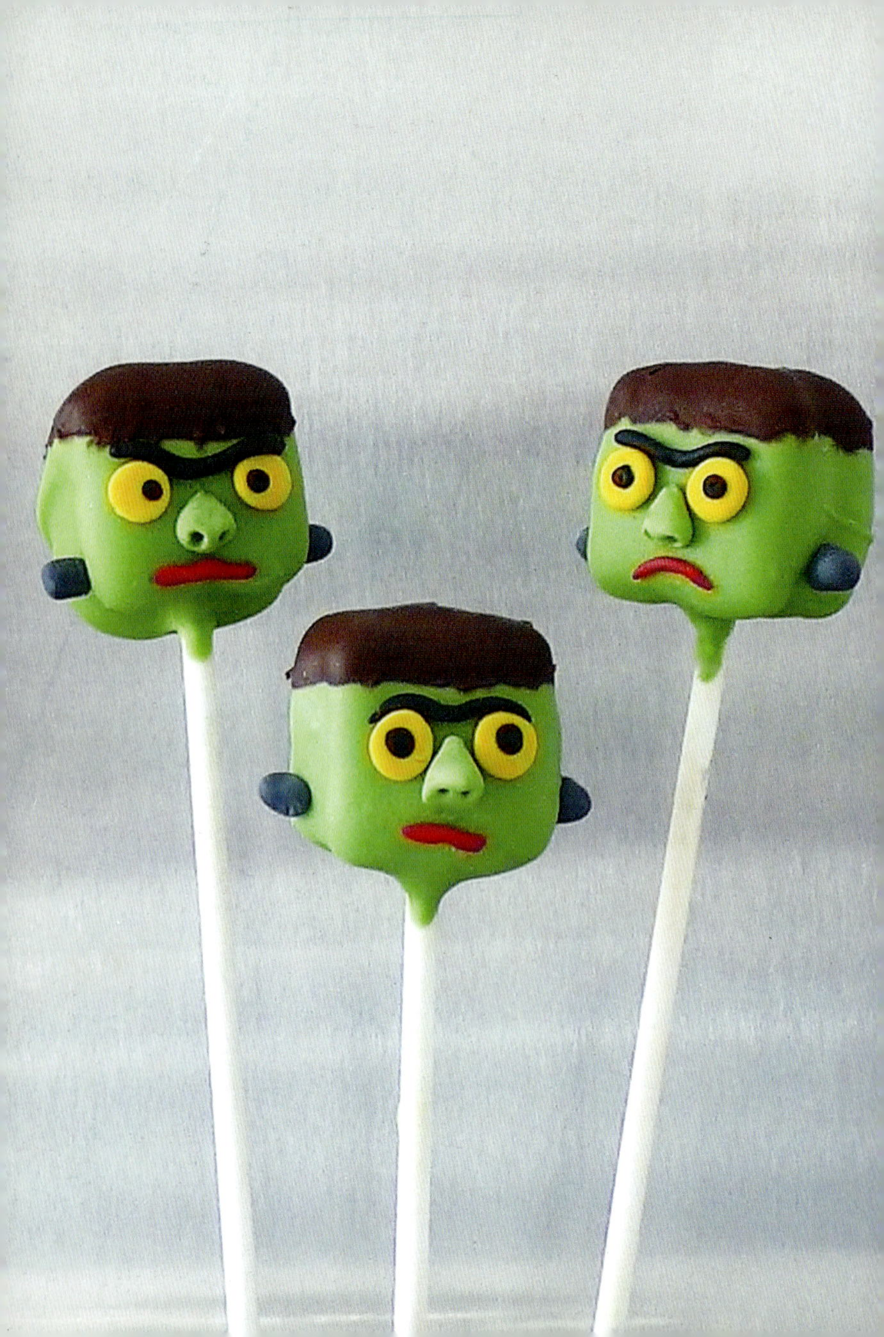

Frankie the Monster

Vanilla Marshmallows and Mini Graham Crackers

Dr. Frankenstein created his fearsome monster, and now you can create your own. Bite into one of these little green marshmallow monsters and you'll be crying out for s'more!

Makes about 35 marshmallow pops.

INGREDIENTS

For the Marshmallows

1/2 cup cold water
3 1/4-ounce packages unflavored gelatin
2 cups sugar
1 cup light corn syrup
1/4 cup cold water
1/4 teaspoon salt
1 tablespoon vanilla extract

For the Dipping and Assembly

35 lollipop sticks
24 ounces green candy coating
6 ounces dark cocoa candy coating
70 mini graham cracker squares

In a large mixing bowl, stir together ½ cup cold water and gelatin. Set aside for about 10 minutes.

In a medium saucepan, mix together sugar, corn syrup, and ¼ cup cold water. Bring to a boil and continue cooking over medium-high heat until a candy thermometer reaches 240°F (116°C). With the blender on high, slowly pour the hot mixture into the gelatin mixture. Add salt and continue to beat on high until hard peaks form. Beat in vanilla and then use a wooden spoon or spatula to scoop the marshmallow into a resealable plastic bag or pastry bag. *You must pipe onto graham crackers immediately (before the marshmallow has a chance to set); see step 1.*

You will need

- Fondant in the following colors: yellow, black, green, red, gray
- Toothpick
- Sharp knife

1. To create the pop, place 1 mini graham cracker face down. Using a pastry bag or resealable plastic bag with a small corner cut out, pipe a small amount of freshly made marshmallow onto the cracker (see page 106). Immediately place a lollipop stick on it as shown.

2. Pipe a small amount of marshmallow on the second cracker and then press that cracker on top of the first cracker as shown. Allow it to set for at least 2 hours.

Frankie the Monster • 107

3.

Dip the set marshmallow-cracker sandwich in green candy coating. Tap gently to get the excess coating off and let dry for at least 30 minutes.

4.

Dip the top of the pop in dark cocoa candy coating to create the monster's hair. Allow the coating to dry for about 10 minutes.

5.

With a small amount of yellow fondant, roll 2 tiny balls for the eyes. Add 2 teensy black fondant dots for the pupils and place them on the monster's face as shown.

6.

Roll a small amount of black fondant into a very thin sausage shape, and place it above the eyes to create a unibrow as shown.

Frankie the Monster • 109

7.

With a small amount of green fondant, create a triangle-shaped nose and apply it under the eyes as shown.

8.

Use the toothpick to create nostrils.

9.

Roll a tiny amount of red fondant into a thin strip and apply it as shown to create the mouth.

10.

Roll a small amount of gray fondant into a cylinder, and use the knife to cut 2 identical bolts. Affix the bolts to each side of the head as shown.

Frankie the Monster • 111

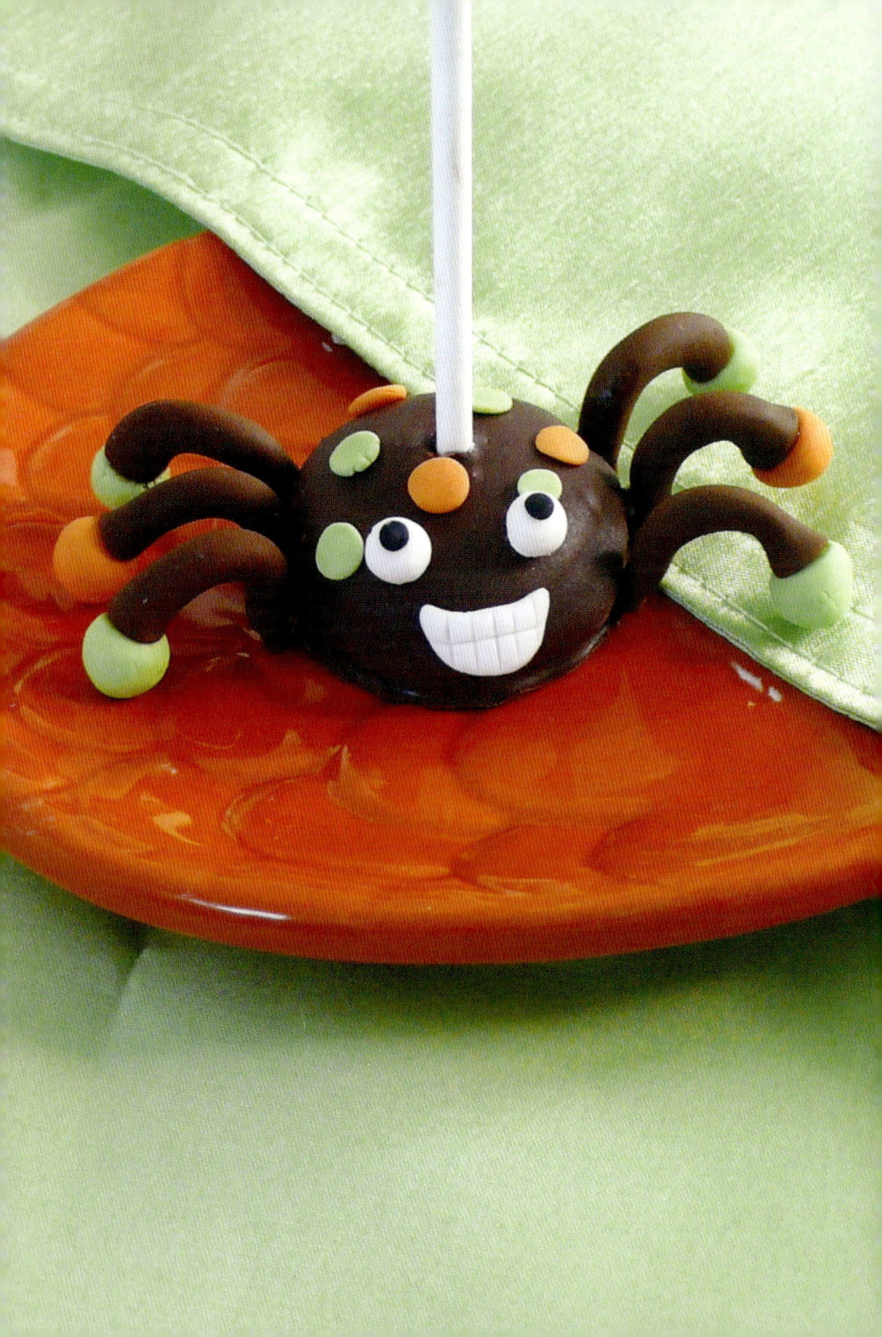

Spotty the Spider
Chocolate Marshmallows and Mini Chocolate Chip Cookies

This little spotted spider looks like he ate a canary — or maybe just a fly. Decorating a bunch of these small spider bites makes for a great birthday or Halloween activity.

Makes about 35 marshmallow pops.

INGREDIENTS

For the Chocolate Marshmallows

½ cup cold water

3 ¼-ounce packages unflavored powdered gelatin

1 cup sugar

⅓ cup light corn syrup

⅓ cup cold water

4 large egg whites at room temperature

Pinch of salt

1 teaspoon vanilla extract

4 tablespoons cocoa powder

For the Dipping and Assembly

35 lollipop sticks

24 ounces dark cocoa candy coating

35 mini chocolate chip cookies

In a small, microwave-safe bowl, stir together ½ cup cold water and gelatin. Set aside.

In a small saucepan, mix together sugar, corn syrup, and ⅓ cup cold water. Bring to a boil and continue cooking over medium-high heat until a candy thermometer registers 245°F (118°C). In the bowl of an electric mixer, beat egg whites on low speed for a few seconds. Add salt, increase the speed of the mixer to high, and beat until the egg whites form a soft peak. Slowly pour the hot syrup into the egg whites while continuing to beat at high speed. Place the bowl with the gelatin in the microwave for about 20 seconds at high power or until the gelatin is completely dissolved. With the mixer still on high, pour the gelatin slowly into the whites. Add vanilla and cocoa powder and continue to whip for about 10 minutes, until the mixture is cool.

Immediately scoop the marshmallow into a resealable plastic bag or pastry bag. *You must pipe onto cookies immediately (before the marshmallow has a chance to set); see step 1.*

You will need

- Fondant in the following colors: green, orange, white, black, dark brown
- Parchment paper
- Toothpick
- Sharp knife

1. Place 1 mini chocolate chip cookie face down on parchment paper. Using a pastry bag or resealable plastic bag with a small corner cut out, pipe a small amount of freshly made chocolate marshmallow onto the cookie. Allow the marshmallow to set for at least 2 hours at room temp.

2. Melt the dark cocoa candy coating in microwave-safe bowl. Use a fork to dip the marshmallow-topped cookie completely in the coating, and carefully place it on a piece of parchment paper.

3.

Immediately insert a lollipop stick in the center of the marshmallow-topped cookie. Let set for 30 minutes at room temp.

4.

Using green and orange fondant, make tiny balls, flatten them into circles, and apply them as shown.

5.

With white fondant, create a crescent-shaped mouth.

6.

With the sharp knife, make indentations to create the teeth. Apply the mouth to the spider as shown.

Spotty the Spider • 117

7.

With a small amount of white fondant, roll 2 tiny balls for the eyes. Add 2 teensy black fondant dots for the pupils and place them on the spider's face as shown.

8.

With dark-brown fondant, create 6 thin, 1-inch-long sausage-shaped legs. Bend them and set-aside.

9.

Make 4 small balls out of green fondant and 2 out of orange fondant. Attach them to one end of each leg, alternating colors as shown.

10.

Affix the legs to the spider's body as shown.

Spotty the Spider • 119

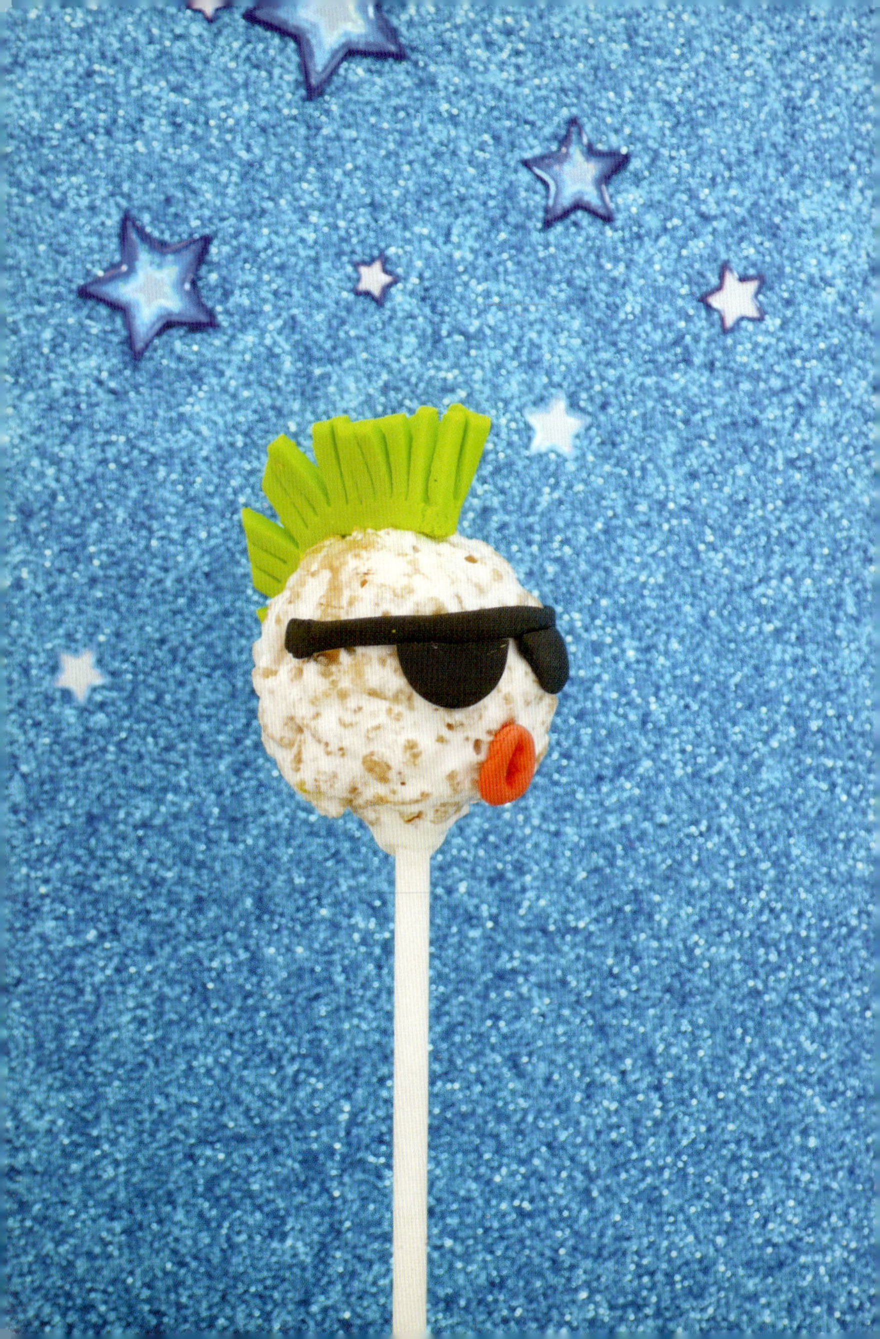

Rock Star

Vanilla Marshmallow Crispy Rice Cereal Treats

This crispy craggy creature is more than just a rock. Boasting a lime-green mohawk and black wraparound sunglasses, this crunchy marshmallow dude really knows how to roll.

Makes about 35 marshmallow pops.

INGREDIENTS

For the Marshmallow Cereal Treat

½ cup cold water

3 ¼-ounce packages unflavored gelatin

2 cups sugar

1 cup light corn syrup

¼ cup cold water

¼ teaspoon salt

1 tablespoon vanilla extract

2 tablespoons unsalted butter

5 cups crispy rice cereal

For the Assembly

35 lollipop sticks

8 ounces white candy coating

In a large mixing bowl, stir together ½ cup cold water and gelatin. Set aside for about 10 minutes.

In a medium saucepan, mix together sugar, corn syrup, and ¼ cup cold water. Bring to a boil and continue cooking over medium-high heat until a candy thermometer reaches 240°F (116°C). With the electric mixer on high, slowly pour the hot sugar mixture into the gelatin mixture. Add salt and continue to beat on high until hard peaks form. Beat in vanilla.

Melt butter in a small saucepan. Add the butter to the marshmallow mixture and stir together with a wooden spoon. Fold in crispy rice cereal until thoroughly blended. Immediately take small mounds of the mixture and roll them into walnut-sized balls. It will be sticky, so you may want to coat your palms with a small amount of vegetable oil first. Place the balls on parchment paper until ready to make your pops.

You will need

- Fondant in the following colors: lime green, black, coral
- Rolling pin
- Sharp knife
- Parchment paper

1. Using the technique on page 9, dip a lollipop stick in melted white candy coating and then insert it in the marshmallow-treat ball. Place on parchment paper and allow to dry completely before decorating (about 10 minutes).

2. Use the rolling pin to roll out lime green fondant.

Rock Star • 123

3.

Use the sharp knife to cut a strip (about 3 X ½ inches).

4.

Cut off 2 corners as shown.

5.

Use the knife to make slits along the length of the fondant as shown.

6.

Fold the fondant over itself and apply it to the pop as shown to create the mohawk. Separate the hair a little with your fingers.

Rock Star • 125

7.

Roll a thin strip of black fondant and flatten it slightly. Apply it halfway around the head as shown.

8.

Roll a small ball of black fondant, flatten it, and cut it in half.

126 • CUTIE POPS

9.

Apply the halves to the head as shown to create sunglasses.

10.

For the mouth, roll a small amount of coral fondant in a sausage shape. Bring the ends together to form an oval. Apply it as shown.

Rock Star • 127

Table of Equivalents

Some of the conversions in these lists have been slightly rounded for measuring convenience.

VOLUME:

U.S.	metric
¼ teaspoon	1.25 milliliters
½ teaspoon	2.5 milliliters
¾ teaspoon	3.75 milliliters
1 teaspoon	5 milliliters
1 tablespoon (3 teaspoons)	15 milliliters
2 tablespoons	30 milliliters
3 tablespoons	45 milliliters
1 fluid ounce (2 tablespoons)	30 milliliters
¼ cup (4 tablespoons)	60 milliliters
⅓ cup	80 milliliters
½ cup	120 milliliters
⅔ cup	160 milliliters
1 cup	240 milliliters
2 cups (1 pint)	480 milliliters
4 cups (1 quart or 32 ounces)	960 milliliters
1 gallon (4 quarts)	3.8 liters

WEIGHT:

U.S.	metric
1 ounce (by weight)	28 grams
1 pound	448 grams
2.2 pounds	1 kilogram

LENGTH:

U.S.	metric
⅛ inch	3 millimeters
¼ inch	6 millimeters
½ inch	12 millimeters
1 inch	2.5 centimeters

OVEN TEMPERATURE:

fahrenheit	celsius
250	120
275	140
300	150
325	160
350	180
375	190
400	200
425	220
450	230
475	240
500	260